Francis Frith's
Suffolk Coast
Photographic Memories

Francis Frith's

Suffolk Coast

Photographic Memories

Roly Smith

www.francisfrith.com

First published in the United Kingdom in 2001 by The Francis Frith Collection.

Hardback Edition Published in 2001 ISBN 1-85937-259-7

Paperback Edition 2005 ISBN 1-85937-610-X

Reprinted in Paperback 2009 ISBN 978-1-85937-610-2

British Library Cataloguing in Publication Data

Francis Frith's Suffolk Coast - Photographic Memories
Roly Smith
ISBN 978-1-85937-610-2

The Francis Frith Collection
Frith's Barn, Teffont,
Salisbury, Wiltshire SP3 5QP
Tel: +44 (0) 1722 716 376
Email: info@francisfrith.co.uk
www.francisfrith.com

Printed and bound in Malta

Front Cover: **Felixstowe, From the Beach 1899** 44513xt

The colour-tinting is for illustrative purposes only, and is not intended to be historically accurate

Suffolk Coast
Photographic Memories

Contents

SUFFOLK

COUNTY MAP c1850

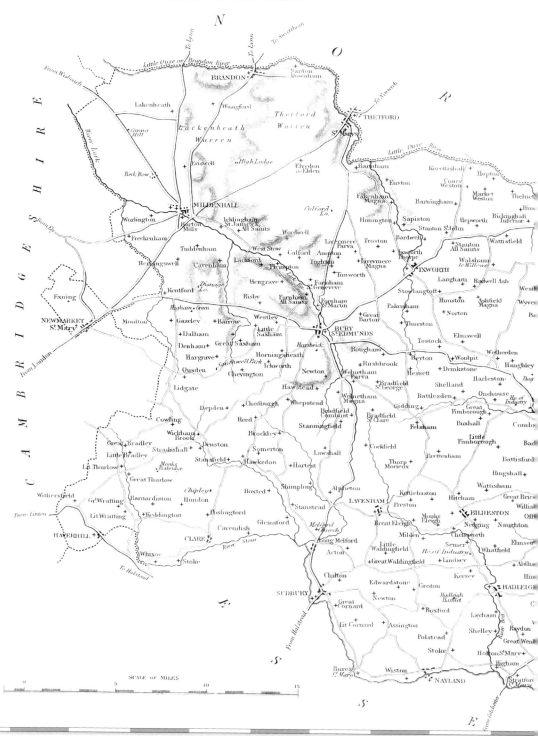

N

O

R

To Lynn
To Lynn
To Swaffham

Little Ouse or Brandon River
BRANDON

Saxton Downham

From Wisbeach

Lakenheath
Wangford

Thetford Warren

To Norwich

THETFORD

River Lark
Ginna Hill

Lockenheath Warren

Little Ouse River

St Marys

Beck Row
Eriswell
High Lodge
Elvedon or Elden
Barnham
Knettishall
Hopton

Euston
Coney Weston
Market Weston
Thelnet

Worlington
MILDENHALL
Iddingham St James
All Saints
Wordwell
Honington
Sapiston
Barningham
Hepworth
Rickinghall Inferior
Hine

Freckenham
Barton Mills

Livermere Parva
Troston
Bardwell
Stanton St John
Stanton All Saints
Wattisfield

Tuddenham
West Stow
Culford
Ampton
Ingham
Livermere Magna
Ixworth Thorpe
Walsham le Willows

Herringswell
Cavenham
Lackford
Flempton
Tamworth
IXWORTH
Langham
Rickwell Ash

Kentford
Disnage La
Hengrave
Fornham St Genevéve
Stowlangtoft
Hunston
Ashfield Magna
Wyves
West

Exning
Higham Green
Risby
Fornham All Saints
Fornham St Martin
Pakenham
Norton
Ba

NEWMARKET St Mary
Moulton
Gazeley
Barrow
Westley
Little Saxham
Great Barton
Thurston
Elmswell
Wetherden

Dalham
Great Saxham
Hardwick
BURY ST EDMUNDS
Rougham
Beyton
Woolpit
Drinkstone
Haughley
Harleston
Dag

Denham
Hargrave
Southwell Park
Ickworth
Newton
Welnetham Parva
Rushbrook
Hessett
Shelland
Ratlesden
Onehouse
Ho. of Industry

Ousden
Chevington
Hawstead
Welnetham Magna
Bradfield St George
Gidding
Great Fimborough
Comb

Lidgate

Depden
Chedburgh
Whepstead
Bradfield Combust
Bradfield St Clare
Felsham
Buxhall
Little Fimborough
Bad

Cowling
Wickham Brook
Denston
Reed
Brockley
Stanningfield
Cockfield
Thorp Morieux
Brettenham
Battisford

Great Bradley
Little Bradley
Stradishall
Somerton
Lawshall
Ringshall

Lt Thurlow
Monks Rushbridge
Stansfield
Hawkedon
Hartest
Alpheton
Kettlebaston
Wattisham
Great Brice
Willish

Withersfield
Great Thurlow
Chipley
Boxted
Stimpling
Preston
Hitcham
BILDESTON
Off

Gr Wratting
Barnardiston
Hundon
Stanstead
LAVENHAM
Monks Eleigh
Nedging
Naughton

HAVERHILL
Lit Wratting
Keddington
Poslingford
Glemsford
Melford Church
Brent Eleigh
Milden
Chelsworth
Semer
Whatfield
Elmset

From Linton
Cavendish
Little Waddingfield
Ho. of Industry
Lindsey
Aldha

Whixoe
CLARE
Stoke
River Stour
Long Melford
Acton
Great Waldingfield
Kersey
HADLEIGH
Hin

To Halstead
Chilton
Edwardstone
Groton
Hadleigh Hamlet

SUDBURY
Great Cornard
Newton
Boxford
Layham
Raydon

Lit Cornard
Assington
Shelley
Great Wen
Holton St Mary
Higham

From Halstead
Polstead
Stoke

Bures St Mary
Wiston
NAYLAND
Stratford St Mary

S
From Colchester

E

SCALE OF MILES

0   5   10   15

4

BREYDON WATER
GREAT YARMOUTH
South Town
Burgh Castle
Belton
Bradwell
Gorleston
Fritton
Ashby Lound Hopton
Herringfleet
Somerleyton Blundeston Corton
Flixton
Ho. of Industry Gunton
Oulton
Kirkley LOWESTOFT
Lake Lothing
Pakefield
Barnby
Mutford Carlton Colville Gisleham
Rushmere
Weston Ellough Henstead
Willingham Sotterley Kessingland
Redisham Shadingfield
Wrentham Binacre
Brampton Frostenden Nth Hales or Covehithe
Stoven
Uggeshall Sth Cove
Sotherton
Wangford
Reydon Easton Bavents
Holton
Ho. of Industry
Blythford Blyburgh SOUTHWOLD
Blythburgh
Wenhaston with Mells Walberswick
Thorington
Hinton

K
L
O

BUNGAY
Mettingham Barsham BECCLES
Ho. of Industry
Shipmeadow Worlingham
Nth Cove
St Johns St Andrew Ringsfield
Ilketshall Ilketshall
Flixton
St Peter St Margaret St Lawrence
Ilketshall Ilketshall
Homersfield
St Cross South Elmham
South Elmham St Michael
South Elmham
Mendham St Margaret
South Elmham All Saints
South Elmham
St Nicholas Rumburgh
South Elmham Spexhall
St James Wissett
Withersdale South Elmham Westhall
Weybread Metfield
Linstead HALESWORTH
Palgrave Fressingfield Parva Chediston
Stuston Syleham Hoxne Cooksey Holton
Thrandeston Broome Wingfield Linstead Huntingfield Blythford
Magna Walpole
Mellis Oakley Denham Cratfield
Yaxley EYE Horham Stradbroke Bramfield
Thornham Braiseworth Wilby Ubbeston
Parva Occold Athelington Laxfield Haveningham
Thornham Redlingfield
Magna Thorndon Bedingfield Brundish Darsham
Stoke Ash All Saints Worlingworth Badingham Peasenhall Westleton
Rushangles Southolt Tannington Sibton Middleton
Brockford Bedfield Yoxford with Fordley
Wetheringsett Saxtead Dennington Bruisyard
Kenton Cransford Rendham Kelsale
Aspall Theberton
Monk Soham Sweffling
DEBENHAM Carlton
Ashfield East Soham FRAMLINGHAM SAXMUNDHAM
Winston Great Leiston
Mickfield Cretingham Kettleburgh Glemham Benhall Sternfield Sizewell
Stonham Framsden Parham Stratford Knodishall
Apsall Pettaugh St Andrew Snape
Earl Monewden Hoo Easton Farnham Sternfield Freston
Stonham Brandeston Little Aldringham
Crowfield Letheringham Glemham Haslewood
Creeting Helmingham Marlesford Aldburgh
St Mary Charsfield Campsea Iken Bay
NEEDHAM Gosbeck Ash Blaxhall
MARKET Ash Bocking Otley Debach Wickham Tunstall ALDBURGH
Coddenham Clopton Market
Helmingstone Swilland Burgh Bredfield Rendlesham Wantisden
House of Boulge Petistree Chillesford
Industry Henley House of Ufford Eyke Sudborne
Barham Grundisburgh Witnesham Industry Melton Butley
Akenham Hasketon Bromeswell ORFORD
Blakenham Culpho
Parva Tuddenham Playford Great Bealings
Whitton Claydon Little WOODBRIDGE
Bramford Westerfield Bealings
Sutton
IPSWICH Capel
Rushmere St Andrew
Martlesham Boyton
Resgrave
Stoke Waldringfield
St Mary Foxhall Brightwell
Belstead Bucklesham Newbourn Shottisham Hollesly
Wherstead Hemly
Nacton Ramsholt
Bentley Freston Levington Kirton Alderton
Ho. of Industry Woolverstone Falkenham Bawdsey
Tattingstone Holbrook Chelmondiston Trimley St Mary
Brantham Harkstead Shotley Trimley St Martin
Erwarton Walton
Felixstow

RIVER STOUR
HARWICH
Landguard Fort

GERMAN OCEAN

River Waveney
To Norwich
River Blyth
River Deben
River Alde
River Ore
Haverghate I.
Orford Ness
Butley River
Aldburgh Bay

5

Dunwich, The Village c1955   D173003

FRANCIS FRITH

Victorian Pioneer

FRANCIS FRITH, founder of the world-famous photographic archive, was a complex and multi-talented man. A devout Quaker and a highly successful Victorian businessman, he was philosophical by nature and pioneering in outlook.

By 1855 he had established a wholesale grocery business in Liverpool, and sold it for the astonishing sum of £200,000, which is the equivalent today of over £15,000,000. Now a very rich man, he was able to indulge his passion for travel. As a child he had pored over travel books written by early explorers, and his fancy and imagination had been stirred by family holidays to the sublime mountain regions of Wales and Scotland. 'What lands of spirit-stirring and enriching scenes and places!' he had written. He was to return to these scenes of grandeur in later years to 'recapture the thousands of vivid and tender memories', but with a different purpose. Now in his thirties, and captivated by the new science of photography,

Frith set out on a series of pioneering journeys up the Nile and to the Near East that occupied him from 1856 until 1860.

Intrigue and Exploration

These far-flung journeys were packed with intrigue and adventure. In his life story, written when he was sixty-three, Frith tells of being held captive by bandits, and of fighting 'an awful midnight battle to the very point of surrender with a deadly pack of hungry, wild dogs'. Wearing flowing Arab costume, Frith arrived at Akaba by camel sixty years before Lawrence of Arabia, where he encountered 'desert princes and rival sheikhs, blazing with jewel-hilted swords'.

He was the first photographer to venture beyond the sixth cataract of the Nile. Africa was still the mysterious 'Dark Continent', and Stanley and Livingstone's historic meeting was a decade into the future. The conditions for picture taking confound belief. He laboured for hours in his wicker dark-room in the sweltering heat of the desert, while the volatile chemicals fizzed dangerously in their trays. Back in London he exhibited his photographs and was 'rapturously cheered' by members of the Royal Society. His reputation as a photographer was made overnight.

Venture of a Life-Time

Characteristically, Frith quickly spotted the opportunity to create a new business as a specialist publisher of photographs. He lived in an era of immense and sometimes violent change. For the poor in the early part of Victoria's reign work was exhausting and the hours long, and people had precious little free time to enjoy themselves. Most had no transport other

than a cart or gig at their disposal, and rarely travelled far beyond the boundaries of their own town or village. However, by the 1870s the railways had threaded their way across the country, and Bank Holidays and half-day Saturdays had been made obligatory by Act of Parliament. All of a sudden the working man and his family were able to enjoy days out and see a little more of the world.

With typical business acumen, Francis Frith foresaw that these new tourists would enjoy having souvenirs to commemorate their days out. In 1860 he married Mary Ann Rosling and set out on a new career: his aim was to photograph every city, town and village in Britain. For the next thirty years he travelled the country by train and by pony and trap, producing fine photographs of seaside resorts and beauty spots that were keenly bought by millions of Victorians. These prints were painstakingly pasted into family albums and pored over during the dark nights of winter, rekindling precious memories of summer excursions.

The Rise of Frith & Co

Frith's studio was soon supplying retail shops all over the country. To meet the demand he gathered about him a small team of photographers, and published the work of

independent artist-photographers of the calibre of Roger Fenton and Francis Bedford. In order to gain some understanding of the scale of Frith's business one only has to look at the catalogue issued by Frith & Co in 1886: it runs to some 670 pages, listing not only many thousands of views of the British Isles but also many photographs of most European countries, and China, Japan, the USA and Canada. By 1890 Frith had created the greatest specialist photographic publishing company in the world, with over 2,000 sales outlets - more than the combined number that Boots and WH Smith have today! The picture on page 9 shows the Frith & Co display board at Ingleton in the Yorkshire Dales (left of window). Beautifully constructed with a mahogany frame and gilt inserts, it could display up to a dozen local scenes.

Postcard Bonanza

The ever-popular holiday postcard we know today took many years to develop. In 1870 the Post Office issued the first plain cards, with a pre-printed stamp on one face. In 1894 they allowed other publishers' cards to be sent through the mail with an attached adhesive halfpenny stamp. Demand grew rapidly, and in 1895 a new size of postcard was permitted called the court card, but there was little room for illustration. In 1899, a year after Frith's death, a new card measuring 5.5 x 3.5 inches became the standard format, but it was not until 1902 that the divided back came into being, so that the address and message could be on one face and a full-size illustration on the other. Frith & Co were in the vanguard of postcard development: Frith's sons Eustace and Cyril continued their father's monumental task, expanding the number of views offered to the public and recording more and more places in Britain, as the coasts and countryside were opened up to mass travel.

Francis Frith had died in 1898 at his villa in Cannes, his great project still growing. The archive he created continued in business for another seventy years. By 1970 it contained over a third of a million pictures showing 7,000 British towns and villages.

Francis Frith's Legacy

Frith's legacy to us today is of immense significance and value, for the magnificent archive of evocative photographs he created provides a unique record of change in the cities, towns and villages throughout Britain over a century and more. Frith and his fellow studio photographers revisited locations many times down the years to update their views, compiling for us an enthralling and colourful pageant of British life and character.

We are fortunate that Frith was dedicated to recording the minutiae of everyday life, for it is this sheer wealth of visual data, the painstaking chronicle of changes in dress, transport, street layouts, buildings, housing, engineering and landscape that captivates us so much today. His remarkable images offer us a powerful link with the past and with the lives of our ancestors.

The Value of the Archive Today

Computers have now made it possible for Frith's many thousands of images to be accessed almost instantly. Frith's images are increasingly used as visual resources, by social historians, by researchers into genealogy and ancestry, by architects and town planners, and by teachers involved in local history projects.

In addition, the archive offers every one of us an opportunity to examine the places where we and our families have lived and worked down the years. Highly successful in Frith's own era, the archive is now, a century and more on, entering a new phase of popularity. Historians consider the Francis Frith Collection to be of prime national importance. It is the only archive of its kind remaining in private ownership. Francis Frith's archive is now housed in an historic timber barn in the beautiful village of Teffont in Wiltshire. Its founder would not recognize the archive office as it is today. In place of the many thousands of dusty boxes containing glass plate negatives and an all-pervading odour of photographic chemicals, there are now ranks of computer screens. He would be amazed to watch his images travelling round the world at unimaginable speeds through internet lines.

The archive's future is both bright and exciting. Francis Frith, with his unshakeable belief in making photographs available to the greatest number of people, would undoubtedly approve of what is being done today with his lifetime's work. His photographs depicting our shared past are now bringing pleasure and enlightenment to millions around the world a century and more after his death.

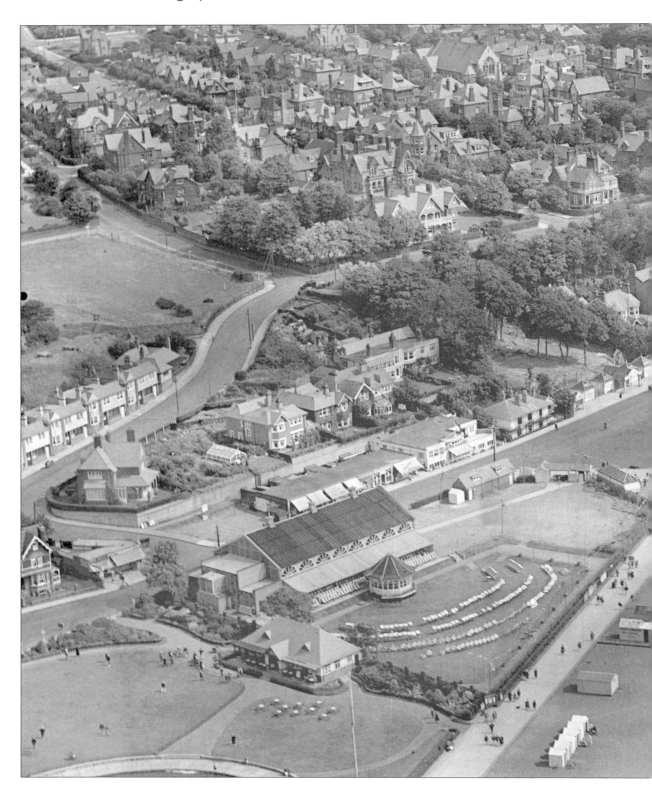

Felixstowe From the Air 1932 AF39279

Suffolk Coast - An Introduction

Describing Suffolk as it was in 1732-43, John Kirby of Wickham Market identified three landscape divisions within his native county. In his book 'The Suffolk Traveller', Kirby split Suffolk into the Sandlands (now usually known as the Sandlings), the Woodlands and the Fielding. The Woodlands were the central claylands from Haverhill to Beccles, where modern 'Barley Barons' have transformed the formerly heavily-wooded landscape into great hedgeless prairies of wheat. Kirby's 'Fielding' was the more open country around Bury St. Edmunds, Newmarket and Mildenhall, where the chalk comes to the surface to create great open spaces like Newmarket Heath, ideal for its famous gallops for racehorses. It is with the Sandlings, the low-lying coastal belt between Felixstowe and Lowestoft and the Rivers Orwell and Waveney, that this book is concerned. Of all Kirby's Georgian topographical divisions, it is the Sandlings which have remained the most naturally beautiful, the most unspoilt and the least changed of all the varied landscapes of Suffolk.

It contains some of the last great lowland heaths in Britain, sweeping down to reed-fringed creeks and extensive salt marshes which are the home of many rare birds. That was the reason why that in 1969, 155 square miles (403 sq km) was designated as the Suffolk Coast and Heaths Area of Outstanding Natural Beauty (AONB). It includes 35 miles (57km) of the Suffolk Heritage Coast, and no less than three National Nature Reserves, the Royal Society for the Protection of Birds' famous Minsmere reserve, and numerous other local nature reserves.

The AONB designation protects this area of heathland, salt marsh and mud flats, all of which are threatened habitats in lowland Britain today. The coast is deeply indented by the slow-flowing estuaries of the Rivers Blyth, Alde, Deben, Orwell and Stour, and is bounded by the low, ever-crumbling sea cliffs and by tidal shingle spits, where the pounding waves of the North Sea seem to be taking away the land with one hand and giving it back with another. At places like Dunwich the low sea cliffs seem to be continually fighting a losing battle against the waves, but their debris is then systematically deposited a few miles further south down the coast at places

like the long shingle spit of Orford Ness, which has significantly altered the course of the River Alde during the period of recorded history.

The Suffolk Coast and Heaths AONB is one of the most important areas for wildlife in Britain. Over 280 species of birds - including the RSPB's 'trademark', the elegant, black-and-white avocet - have been recorded on the RSPB's Minsmere reserve, near Dunwich. Havergate Island, near Orford, is another RSPB reserve, where avocets are joined by short-eared owl and marsh harriers, which quarter in the wind over the waving reeds of the salt marshes.

The low-lying coastal hinterland contains some of England's last remaining areas of ancient lowland heath, such as Dunwich Common. This is perhaps the best surviving example of one of Kirby's Sandlings, which were grazed by enormous flocks of sheep in medieval times. Today, they are still the home of all three species of heather, gorse and broom, and of the nationally-rare nightjar; the Dartford warbler and several species of heathland butterflies also find refuge here. Other former heaths, such as those at Rendlesham and Tunstall, have been colonised by the alien, regimented conifers of the Forestry Commission, and now provide a tiny fraction of the habitats for wildlife that they once did.

The Vikings knew this heavily-indented coastline intimately, and it is certain that their predatory dragon-bowed longships must have nosed far inland on the estuaries. At Sutton Hoo, just to the east of Woodbridge, one of the richest archaeological finds ever made in Britain took place in 1939. A miraculously-undisturbed Saxon ship burial overlooking the Deben estuary provided a glittering horde of artefacts made from gold, silver and precious stones, all of which are now on display in the British Museum. The burial echoes almost exactly that described in the Dark Age masterpiece 'Beowulf', and the best guess seems to be that the Sutton Hoo burial was of the Anglo-Saxon King of East Anglia, Raedwald.

Architecturally, the most impressive towns are Aldeburgh, where the red-brick and flint-faced half-timbered Tudor Moot Hall still dominates the mainly Georgian High Street, and unspoilt Woodbridge, further inland at the tidal limit of the River Deben, where the Old Tide Mill is still dependent on the rising and falling of the North Sea. The former maltings at Snape, near Aldeburgh, have become famous for the annual Aldeburgh Music Festival, established by composer Benjamin Britten and singer Peter Pears in 1948, which today attracts internationally-known artists and admiring

and appreciative audiences to the magnificent converted Victorian red-brick buildings.

Orford is an even-earlier settlement on the River Alde, now cut off from the sea by the shingle spit of Orford Ness, but once an important medieval port. The beautifully preserved three-turreted castle keep, built by Henry II to control his East Anglian interests, is a fine viewpoint across the Ness towards its red-and-white lighthouse. As mentioned above, it was the gradual growth of Orford Ness which sealed Orford's fate as a port, cutting it off from the sea. In 1722, the author and journalist Daniel Defoe was able to report that Orford was 'now decayed. The sea daily throws up more land, so it is a seaport no longer'. Southwold is also dominated by its white lighthouse tower, while the flint-faced cottages of Walberswick, across the Blyth estuary, have enjoyed a new lease of life with the coming of the holiday trade. The former township of Dunwich, south of Southwold, has not fared so well; it was another victim of the remorseless sea. An important East Coast port in Saxon and Norman times, it once boasted a population of over 5,000 souls and three churches. But a fierce storm in 1326 resulted in the diversion of the River Blyth northwards, effectively sealing Dunwich's fate. The crashing North Sea breakers did the rest, leaving a few solitary ruins and gravestones near the cliff edge as mute reminders of the town's former glories.

The threat of Napoleonic invasion was the original reason for the construction of the many circular Martello towers, which still punctuate the shoreline of the Suffolk coast. Built during the early 19th century, these defensive structures no longer have a military use, and many have been converted

into unusual homes. A much later, and more incongruous, addition to the landscape was the ugly, concrete block structure of the Sizewell B Nuclear Power Station, on the coast east of Leiston.

The photographs in this book range from the late 19th century to the mid 20th century, and the scenes they depict show a Suffolk coast before the days of mass motoring and tourism. Fishermen still go about their business on uncrowded quays, and the broad canvas sails of old-fashioned East Anglian and Thames sailing barges still catch the wind in the background. Resorts like Lowestoft, Felixstowe and Southwold - all former fishing villages where once fleets of fishing boats harvested the riches of the North Sea - were, however, already starting to attract large numbers of holidaymakers. The Frith collection shows photographs of them strolling along the esplanades down to the piers which were the centres of entertainment then, and often the only places where working-class people actually went to the theatre. Donkey rides on the beach were a highlight for the children, along with ever-popular Punch and Judy shows, sticky-sweet seaside rock and candy floss.

Colourful pink-washed and thatched cottages decorate the few villages within the area, and their spacious greens remind us of a time before fast-moving traffic dominated the roads, and when life itself seemed to move at a much slower pace. Villagers, especially children, stand around fascinated by Frith's cameraman, and many seem to be posing especially for the photographer. It was in those days that Suffolk gained its epithet, 'sleepy', and these photographs seem to provide ample evidence, if any was needed.

Aldeburgh, The Moot Hall 1894 33360

The Tudor red brick and half-timbered Moot Hall has dominated Aldeburgh's Main Street for 500 years, and is a reminder of the time of the town's greatest prosperity as a sea port, during the 16th century, before the River Alde was cut off by the sea by the growth of Orford Ness. The building was heavily restored in 1855, and the sundial, visible on the gable end, dates from 1650.

Aldeburgh, Main Street, 1901 46697

Another view of the Moot Hall opposite Jay's Family Hotel; we are looking down the Main Street. Note the elaborate half-timbering and decorated barge boards on the end of the Moot Hall, and the horse and cart in the street.

Aldeburgh
High Street 1894 33362
This view of a deserted
High Street looks
towards the old Market
Square, at a time when
horse-drawn transport
was the rule of the day.
Awnings protect the
shops on the right-hand
side of the photograph
from the fading effects
of the sun.

**Aldeburgh
Old Market Square,
1929** *82977*
By this time, the internal
combustion engine was
beginning to make its
mark on the Aldeburgh
street scene. This view of
the Old Market Square
shows an approaching
single-decker bus on
Route 3A, Ward's Garage
down the street on the
left, and tradesmens'
vans parked in the
square.

▲ **Aldeburgh**
The Town Steps 1906 56826
The Town Steps, leading down to the old town
and sea front, are still an attractive feature of
Aldeburgh. Note the East Coast roofing speciality
of pantiles on many of the old cottages either
side of the Steps.

◄ **Detail From:**
Aldeburgh
The Town Steps 1906 56826

Aldeburgh, The Town Steps c1960 A28088
Holidaymakers make their way down The Steps to the sea front at Aldeburgh, while others take a rest halfway up the steep flight. The pushchair and bicycle with basket on the left of the photograph help to date this picture.

Aldeburgh, The Parade 1906 56816
Hats, long black dresses and parasols were the order of the day for the ladies taking their exercise along Aldeburgh's Parade. C Harling was offering boating and bathing from his wooden hut in the right foreground, while lined up along the beach are typical East Coast sailing boats.

▲ **Aldeburgh**
The Parade 1909 62011
A sailor home on leave from his ship pauses for
the photographer as he takes his small daughter
for a walk along the Parade. Perhaps the lady on
the white donkey on his left is his wife. A bearded
and capped bystander on the right looks on.

◄ **Detail From:**
Aldeburgh
The Parade 1909 62011

Aldeburgh, The Beach 1929 82969
A pipe-smoking man and his two lady companions enjoy the sun and the sea as they sit out on the beach benches.
Note the quizzical expression from the sailor-capped old sea dog sitting at the next bench, and the winding gear
to haul in the boats which line the beach.

Aldeburgh, The River Alde 1901 46709
This fine view over the mast of a sailing boat across the estuary of the River Alde looks towards the Martello Tower
south of Slaughden in the distance. This was the northernmost of the Martello Towers built in defence against the
threat of Napoleon in the 1800s. Note the anchor on the beach in the foreground.

◄ **Aldeburgh
Slaughden Quay
1906** 56821
Slaughden was once
a prosperous village
to the south of
Aldeburgh, but coastal
erosion has gradually
taken its relentless
effect: by 1959, only
the foundations of its
houses were visible
at low tide. This
photograph shows
a fine line-up of
moored sailing boats.

◀ **Aldeburgh**
Mill Mansion 1903 50434
Converted from a post windmill, the white-painted, copper-topped Mill Mansion is a well-known feature of Aldeburgh, which at one time boasted two windmills. As their former use became redundant, many East Anglian windmills like this have been converted to houses.

▲ **Aldeburgh**
The Martello Tower c1960
A28100
The clover-leaf walls of the Martello Tower at the entrance to the estuary of the River Alde south of Slaughden have withstood the worst of the North Sea weather since the early 19th century, when the tower was built to combat the threat of Napoleonic invasion. It was the northernmost Martello Tower of the many which dot the East Coast.

◀ **Aldeburgh**
The Golf House
1896 38673
Aldeburgh's thatched and mock-Tudor Golf Clubhouse, seen here soon after it was built, attempts to mimic the town's most famous landmark, the Moot Hall, with its half-timbering and red brick walls.

◀ **Alderton**
The School c1950

A342008

The red-brick village school at Alderton is typical of many East Anglian village schools; they catered for the educational needs of the village children before they had to travel probably to nearby Woodbridge for their secondary studies.

Alderton
The Street c1950 A342004
The main street of the small village of Alderton, inland from Bawdsey on Hollesley Bay, on a quiet summer's day. The white-walled Swan Inn (centre) was owned by the famous Ipswich brewers, Cobbolds, while the Crown Inn, opposite, was run by Tolly. The two brewers were later to combine to create Tolly-Cobbold.

Bawdsey, The Victoria Inn 1894 34808
Bawdsey, seen here from the shore looking towards the Victoria Inn on the seafront, is perhaps best known for the first radar research station. It was set up at The Manor in 1936, and was used extensively to pick up raiding Luftwaffe aircraft during the Battle of Britain in 1940.

Bawdsey
The Manor 1899
43243
The flamboyant mock-Tudor Manor House was a newly-built addition to the village when this photograph was taken. It was built by Sir Cuthbert Quilter in 1886. The first radar research station later moved here from Orfordness in May 1936.

◀ **Carlton Colville
The Church c1955**
C508004
The fine, plain, flint-faced tower of Carlton Colville's church dates from the Perpendicular period, and is typical of many East Anglian parish churches. The wealth won from the wool of the region's sheep ranches during the Middle Ages gives many village churches the air of much more important places.

◄ **Carlton Colville
The Street c1955**
C508001
Carlton Colville is a small, undistinguished village just off the A146 to the south-west of Lowestoft. This photograph shows the sign for the village pub, The Bell, on the left, opposite a row of terraced cottages.

▼ **Carlton Colville
Interior of the Parish
Church c1955** C508012
The simple, whitewashed nave of the parish church, looking up from the finely-decorated medieval font on the right. The barrel-beamed roof looks down on the memorial to the village's dead from the two World Wars on the left of the photograph.

◄ **Carlton Colville
The Hall c1955** C508010
The Hall at Carlton Colville looks out on the village green, where black and white Friesian dairy cattle peacefully graze. Note the fine old barn to the right of the Hall.

◄ **Corton, The Beach c1960** C513012
A father and son, probably from the Rogerson's Holiday Camp seen in photograph No C513010, take a walk along the low cliffs of the beach. The ugly radio or radar masts in the background are a common feature of this stretch of the Suffolk coast.

◀ **Corton, The Rogerson Hall Holiday Camp Main Path c1960** C513010

The east coast could be said to be the home of the holiday camp, and one of the earliest was at Rogerston Hall at Corton, a small village north of Lowestoft. In this photograph, two young holidaymakers dash up the Main Path between rose bush borders to join their parents in the single-storey, whitewashed chalets.

▼ **Covehithe The Church 1896** 38642

The fine medieval church of St. Andrew must have been one of the finest in Suffolk before it was partly demolished during the Civil War. But in 1672, a smaller church (just visible behind the ivy-clad arch) was built inside the roofless and windowless nave, using materials from the older church.

◀ **Dunwich The Church Ruins 1909**

62048

The tower and nave of All Saints Parish Church. The church collapsed into the sea in about 1920, and nothing now remains except for a few scattered pieces of masonry.

Dunwich, The Beach 1909 62044

The story of the demise of Dunwich, in medieval times a prosperous port until the ravages of the North Sea gradually demolished its soft, sandy cliffs, is one of the most romantic of the Suffolk Coast. There were still substantial remains of the parish church on the clifftop above the beach tents when this photograph was taken.

Dunwich, Lovers' Walk 1909 62045
This is a romantic path down to the ever-encroaching sea at Dunwich. Many such secluded and tree-lined paths
earned the country epithet 'Lovers' Lane' or 'Lovers' Walk'.

Dunwich, The Beach c1955 D173001
The concrete blocks on the right were part of the coastal defences during the Second World War, designed to stop Nazi tanks from landing. In the background, the low cliffs of Dunwich continue to crumble away, as they have for centuries.

Dunwich, The Village c1955 D173003
A band of excited children, spades in hand, rush back through the village from the beach at Dunwich with their latest finds. In the background, the Berney Arms watches over what is left of the once-busy town.

Suffolk Coast - Photographic Memories

▼ **Dunwich, The Franciscan Priory 1909** 62049

The romantic, ivy-covered ruins of the Franciscan Priory are now the most substantial building left of the medieval Dunwich. The town's fate was sealed on a stormy night in 1326 when tons of sand and shingle were swept across the harbour mouth, cutting it off from the sea.

▼ **Dunwich, Minsmere c1955** D173021

Minsmere is probably the most famous of all the Royal Society for the Protection of Birds' reserves. But caravans and tents were still allowed to park haphazardly along the coast when this photograph was taken. The 1,500-acre reserve, at the mouth of the Minsmere River, is probably best-known for the return of its elegant waders, the black-and-white avocets, which came back to the reserve after an absence of nearly a century in the 1940s.

▲

Felixstowe Beach Donkeys 1891
29038

For Victorian children at the turn of the last century, a donkey ride on the beach was a highlight of their seaside holiday. Here the bowler-hatted custodian waits for his first customers of the day, in front of one of Felixstowe's grand hotels; a white-painted tradesman's handcart, which appears to be that of a cutler, stands centre left.

◄ **Felixstowe**
The Esplanade 1893 32240
Weatherboarded walls, verandahs and balconies characterise the sea-front buildings of Felixstowe. The town was a genteel seaside resort built around a wide, shingle bay which offered excellent, safe bathing. This photograph was taken before the concrete promenade was constructed in 1902 (see also photograph No 82935).

Felixstowe
West Beach 1899 44514
Holidaymakers are strolling and enjoying themselves in the bright summer sunshine.
The two bearded gentlemen in the left foreground are carrying towels, so they are
evidently on their way for a bathe off the shingle beach.

Felixstowe
The Promenade 1904 51251
By 1904, the two-mile-long concrete promenade at Felixstowe had been constructed, offering a pleasant walkway between the gardens of the hotels on the left and the shingle beach on the right of this photograph. Note the gas street lamps, and the delivery wagon outside the hotel in the centre of the picture.

Suffolk Coast - Photographic Memories

▼ **Felixstowe, The Golf Links 1896** 38684
The tiny clubhouse on Felixstowe's bracing golf links is backed by the solid circular structure of a Martello tower, built like the many others along the Suffolk coast in defence of the realm against Napoleonic invasion in the early 19th century.

▼ **Felixstowe, From the Pier 1906** 54637
This view shows the series of groynes or breakwaters which divide up the shingle beach of the resort. The pier had only been constructed two years before this photograph was taken, so this was a novel view at the time; we are looking towards Convalescent Hill, which climbs up from the pierhead.

▲ **Felixstowe The Pier 1907** 58974
Felixstowe's magnificent wooden pier was one of the longest in the country, extending half a mile out into the North Sea. It was also later equipped with electric trams and with shelters for anglers and sunbathers. Note the horsedrawn carriages in the foreground.

◀ **Felixstowe, Behind the The Beach 1907** 58975
A party of children wearing hats and smocks seem to be setting up a picnic on the area of green behind the beach. Wooden bathing huts can be seen on the right of the photograph, with the newly-built wooden pier running off the right.

Felixstowe
The Beach 1907 58958
Fashions in bathing costumes have changed markedly since this photograph was taken. The Edwardians favoured large hats and long dresses for the ladies, and even the children paddling in the waves seem to modern eyes to be well wrapped up against the biting North Sea winds. Prominent in the middle distance, centre, is the ornate bandstand on the Promenade.

Suffolk Coast - Photographic Memories

▼ **Felixstowe, The Zigzag 1906** 54648

This is a rare photograph, for it shows in the foreground two goat carts, designed for use by children. The billys must have been very well behaved! In the background is Felixstowe's famous Zigzag walkway down the cliff to the seafront. The shadows of the gables of the range of wooden bathing huts can be seen on the right.

▼ **Felixstowe, Convalescent Hill 1907** 58961

Convalescent Hill, leading down to the beach, took its name from the Suffolk Convalescent Home situated on the cliff above. The bracing sea air at Felixstowe and the other east coast resorts made them much favoured at the time as places for invalids as they convalesced after their illnesses.

▲ **Felixstowe The Gardens and the Cliff Hotel 1907**
58964

The balconies and porticoes of the Cliff Hotel made it one of the grandest on the town's elegant Edwardian seafront. It is seen here in all its glory with a trio of holidaymakers and their dog enjoying the sunshine in the seafront Spa Gardens on the right of the picture.

◄ **Felixstowe
The Ferry 1907** 58987
The ferry, seen
here in the middle
distance, carries foot
passengers across
the Stour and Orwell
Estuaries to Halfpenny
Pier at Harwich, across
the border in Essex.
The pier in the Essex
town got its unusual
name because when
the ferry first opened,
the fare to Felixstowe
was one halfpenny!

Felixstowe
The Promenade 1929 82935
Compare this photograph with photograph No 32240, which was taken from the identical spot in 1893.
By now, motor cars are using the concrete roadway, the seafront gardens have been laid out, and gas
street lighting installed. The balconied building on the extreme left, once a hotel, is now the Empire Café.

Suffolk Coast - Photographic Memories

▼ **Felixstowe, The Promenade 1929** 82939
Fashions have changed, but the bracing qualities of a walk along the Promenade were just as efficacious as they had always been, as this photograph shows. Note the mother with her 'flapper'-style dress and daughter on the right.

▼ **Felixstowe, Hamilton Road c1950** F16025
The town of Felixstowe grew up as a holiday resort with the coming of the railway around 1900. In later years it has expanded enormously to be one of the busiest container ports in Europe. But when this photograph was taken in one of the main commercial streets, the town was still largely dependent on its holiday trade.

▲ **Felixstowe, Bay Road c1950** F16032
By this time, Felixstowe's reputation as a leading holiday resort was well established. This view of Bay Road, which looks towards the Pier on the left and the white-painted Pier Pavilion on the right, also shows that the motor car had well and truly arrived. Performing daily at the Pier Pavilion at the time was the Jerry Allen Septet.

◄ **Felixstowe, The Gardens and Amusement Park c1955**

F16041

The great steel structure of the rollercoaster ride at the Amusement Park on the left dominates this photograph taken from the Spa Gardens. Billy Butlin's Amusement Park totally changed the aspect of the southern part of the town, which stretches down to Landguard Point on the Orwell estuary.

Kessingland
The Beach c1955
K137017

Suffolk Coast - Photographic Memories

▼ **Kessingland, The Beach c1955** K137005
Caravans were the scourge of the Suffolk coast in the 1950s and 1960s, as we can see here. In those days, they were allowed to park right up to the shingle beach, allowing visitors to step right out from their mobile homes onto the beach.

▼ **Kessingland, Beach Road c1955** K137022
Kessingland lies on the Suffolk coast off the A17 about midway between Lowestoft and Southwold. Like many other Suffolk coastal villages, it was originally a small fishing village - hence the name of the pub, The Sailor's Home, in the left background. But the shingle beach later became popular with boaters and bathers.

▲ **Kessingland Church Road c1955**
K137023
Ivy's wooden-walled store on the right apparently sold everything, and the little girl outside is trying her hand at the ever-popular bubble-gum machine.

◄ **Kessingland**
The Beach c1955

K137033

The wide shingle bank of the beach is always popular with boaters, but the little girl making her way up the bank is more intent on what she has caught with her bucket and spade. This lovely summer photograph was taken at the height of the resort's popularity.

◄ **Leiston, Main Street 1922** 72580
Much of Leiston (pronounced Lace-tn) is a model village constructed by the Garrett family; they owned the Leiston Iron Works, where Richard Garrett produced a famous portable steam engine and threshing machine. This is a view of the Barclays Bank building in the main street.

◄ Kessingland
The Sea Wall c1965
K137037

These leather-clad, winkle-picker-shoed lads sitting on the sea wall would probably describe themselves in the parlance of the day as 'rockers'. Their gleaming motorbikes are parked on the left, but their eyes are on the (probably female) occupants of the white-painted Wave Crest Café.

▼ Leiston, Main Street
1922 72578

At this time, a young lad could walk with impunity down the centre of the road, carrying his mum's shopping. Leiston is situated just inland from Sizewell, on the road to Saxmundham.

◄ Leiston, The Abbey
1929 82978

The brick and flint remains of the Premonstratensian abbey lie to the north of the town, and are probably the most extensive monastic remains in the county. Originally founded at nearby Minsmere, the abbey was rebuilt on its present site in 1388-9. The Georgian house inside the ruins is now used as a diocesan retreat.

Suffolk Coast - Photographic Memories

▼ **Leiston, High Street c1960** L33015
Shop signs dominate this view of the mainly Georgian High Street, which unusually for Suffolk winds up quite a steep hill. Note the awnings and sun shields of Baker Brothers grocery shop, on the left.

▼ **Leiston, High Street c1955** L33032
This view looks in the opposite direction to photograph No L33015. The Leiston Abbey Press, on the right, also had branches at Aldeburgh and Saxmundham, and like so many printers of the day, was also a stationer and publisher of local literature.

▲ **Lowestoft St John's Church and the Vicarage 1891** 28373
The church of St John is an impressive late 15th-century building, with a fine, 120-foot spire, which is set aside from the elegant piered nave arcade, as at Southwold and Blythburgh. This photograph also shows the adjacent vicarage on the left.

◄ **Lowestoft, London Road South 1896**

37925

Another view of St John's Church, this time from the London Road, showing on the right a coach and pair making its stately way along the street, driven by a top-hatted coachman wielding a very long whip.

Lowestoft, The South Pier from the Sands 1896 37936
This is an archetypal late Victorian seaside scene. Deckchairs, donkey rides and, in the background, the South Pier with its gabled Pavilion, make up the picture, while the holidaymakers are, as usual, well-wrapped-up against the biting North Sea breezes.

◀ **Lowestoft
The South Pier
Pavilion 1921** 71694
The Pavilion on
the South Pier was
an ornate, gabled
building, complete
with two-tiered
balconies and a
bandstand in front.
Holidaymakers are
enjoying both the sun
and the band.

◀ **Lowestoft**
The South Pier Reading Room and the Yacht Basin 1896 37938
The broad-sailed East Anglian barges lie at rest in the harbour, while an important-looking figure, who could well be the harbourmaster, sets out in a small boat in the bottom left-hand corner. The Pier Pavilion is in the background.

Lowestoft ▶
The Low Light from Mariner's Score 1921
71704
The unique series of parallel lanes which run steeply down from Lowestoft's High Street to the shore are known as 'scores', perhaps because they were scoured or cut out between the closely-packed buildings. The steep steps of Mariner's Score lead down through flint walls towards the distant Low Light, one of the town's two lighthouses.

◀ **Lowestoft, Rough Seas 1922** 72506
Lowestoft, standing on Britain's most easterly point, has fought a long and not always successful battle against the ravages of the North Sea. A total of £750,000 went into concrete and steel sea defences between 1903 and 1949, and evidence of this work can be seen here, where bystanders appear to be inspecting their performance.

**Lowestoft
The Esplanade c1955**

L105086

The motor car has well and truly arrived on the Lowestoft scene. This view of the Esplanade has the Claremont Pier in the background. Surrounded by cars in the centre of the picture is the bowling green and pavilion, an essential part of the holiday for many visitors.

**Orford, The Village
1909** 62016
This view of the
deserted village square
shows the Castle in
the distance and Ye
Old White Hart Inn, the
white-walled building
on the right. Orford was
a prosperous medieval
port which declined
as the shingle spit of
Orford Ness grew, which
gradually cut it off from
the sea.

▲ **Orford**

The Castle 1909 62018

Orford Castle, the most impressive medieval building on the Suffolk coast, was built by Henry II in 1165, and shows the importance of the port to the realm at the time. Although only the great circular keep remains today, this view shows the remains of the other earthworks and walls which once protected it.

Orford, The Castle ▶
1937 88244
Orford Castle's 90-feet-high keep was of a revolutionary, circular construction, buttressed by three projecting square turrets which are equally spaced around it. The keep has three floors, a basement and two halls, and is constructed from the local flint with dressed sandstone quoins and windows.

▲ **Orford, The River Ore 1937** 88248
North of the village of Orford, the river as it flows down from Aldeburgh is known as the Alde, but south of the village it is called the Ore. This view shows the foreshore as the River Ore runs down towards Havergate Island, now an RSPB bird reserve.

◄ **Orford, The King's Head and the Church c1950** 020029
This photograph shows the ruined tower of the 14th-century church of St Bartholemew. But note photograph No O20084, taken after the restoration of the tower ten years later. The King's Head public house on the left is one of the oldest pubs in Orford, dating back to Tudor times.

◀ **Orford, The Quay c1950** 020036
The Quay is all that remains of the once-prosperous seaport of Orford, cut off now from the North Sea by the growth of Orford Ness. Some trade must have been still going on at this time, as is witnessed by the crane derrick.

◀ **Orford, The Village c1950** 020042
The shopkeeper and his assistant on the right peer out inquisitively from their shop doorway at the photographer, as does the motorist who has just parked his Vauxhall opposite. Note the fenced-off village water pump in the centre of the road.

▼ **Orford, Yachting at The Quay c1960** 020095
A former wartime landing craft, AWRE No 3 (centre), has been adapted to serve as a ferry for foot passengers crossing the Alde to get to Orford Ness. In the background, yachts are enjoying the sheltered waters created by the obstructed harbour.

◀ **Orford, The Church c1960** 020084
Taken from an almost identical spot as picture No O20029, this photograph shows the newly-restored tower of the parish church of St Bartholomew, with the King's Head public house on the left. The trees in the front garden of the bay-windowed house on the right have grown, and a television aerial has been erected on the chimney.

▼ Orford, The King's Head and Post Office c1960 020071

This view shows the opposite end of the King's Head pub, and also the pantile-roofed Post Office on the right. The motorist has just bought a carton of milk from Taylor's Milk and Fruit Shop on the left.

▼ Orford, The Crown and Castle Hotel c1960 020083

The Crown and Castle, at the top of the village near the castle, is one of Orford's oldest hostelries, dating back to the town's heyday in Tudor times, as shown by its originally half-timbered construction. By the time this photograph was taken, it was a Trust House Hotel, recognised by both the AA and RAC.

▲ Orford, The Square c1965 020100

Compare this view of Orford's Square with that shown looking in the opposite direction in picture No 62016, taken in 1909. The road is now metalled and cars are parked haphazardly along the street. An interesting shop front is on the right - the Butley Oysterage. Butley is a small village on the River Butley about three miles inland from Orford, well-known for its seafood.

◀ **Shotley Gate, The Village c1955** S581011
Shotley is a small village on the promontory between the Orwell and Stour estuaries, and is perhaps best known for Shotley Gate, the home of the naval training base HMS 'Ganges' until 1977. This view shows Peter Coulson's tobacconists shop on the extreme right, and an old thatched house in the centre.

Suffolk Coast - Photographic Memories

Shotley, The Village ▶
c1955 S580001
This photograph shows the rural nature of this part of East Suffolk. Stooks of corn are stacked in the field on the left, while in the distance, standing on its spur, can be seen the towerless parish church, which dates from c1300.

◄ **Shotley Gate**
The Bristol Arms
c1955 S581005
The famous Ipswich
brewing company of
Cobbold supplied the
ale for the Bristol Arms,
a popular hostelry for
trainee sailors at HMS
'Ganges' at Shotley Gate
for many years. The
double-decker Eastern
National bus parked in
front advises: 'Say CWS
and Save'.

Suffolk Coast - Photographic Memories

▼ **Shotley Gate, The Pier c1955** S581003
Lifeboats from HMS 'Ganges' line the pier. In the left middle distance can be seen a naval gunboat, anchored in the harbour, while the cranes and larger ships of Harwich Harbour are just visible over the estuary to the extreme right.

▼ **Shotley Gate, General View c1955** S581006
A view from the sea, possibly from the Pier. HMS 'Ganges' was closed in 1977, but the training tradition was maintained when in 1981 it became the Eurosports Village, a residential sports training complex.

▲ **Shotley Gate General View c1965** S581001
A Harwich ferry, probably bound for Esbjerg or the Hook of Holland, passes the Shotley Gate Pier.
A naval ship can just be seen anchored behind the pier.

◄ Sizewell
The Hall c1955 S582002
The mock-Tudor
mansion of Sizewell
Hall lies just outside
this small village,
which lies between
Thorpeness and
Dunwich on the
Suffolk coast. Note the
classical discus thrower
on the pedestal in the
foreground, and the
fine trees which shade
the lawns.

◄ **Sizewell**
The Coastguard
Station c1955 S582003
Sizewell was once
notorious for its
smuggling activities. In
one night here during
the 18th century,
a staggering 8,000
gallons of contraband
gin were landed. The
Coastguard Station,
seen here on the
right, was built partly
to counter these
nefarious activities.

◄ Sizewell
**From the Gardens
of Sizewell Hall c1965**
S582001
This view shows the beautiful and remote Suffolk coast, now a designated Area of Outstanding Beauty and followed by the Suffolk Coast long distance path, as seen from the balustraded gardens of Sizewell Hall.

▼ Sizewell
The Benthills c1955
S582004
The Benthills is the name given to the grassy area behind the seawall at Sizewell. A wooden tea hut, proudly flying its flag, caters for visiting holidaymakers in season.

◄ Sizewell
**The Nuclear Power
Station c1960** S582041
Sizewell is perhaps best-known for its nuclear power station, photographed here soon after its construction. This was the first of two power stations on the site, which produced enough electricity into the National Grid to power a city the size of Bristol. The grey concrete bulk of the controversial water-cooled station still dominates the coast for many miles.

**Southwold
High Street 1891** 28352
Two Southwold
'characters' stand on the
left of a deserted High
Street. Standing on a
cliff top overlooking the
North Sea, Southwold
is virtually an island, cut
off from the mainland
by Buss Creek, which
takes its name from
the 'busses' or herring
fishing boats which
once were moored in it.

**Southwold
East Green 1893** 32185
Southwold consists of
seven 'greens' running
off the High Street.
The theory is that after
a disastrous fire had
devastated the town in
1659, the townspeople
decided that to prevent
it happening again,
they would group the
houses around these
open spaces. The cast
iron notice in the
foreground lays down
the regulations affecting
the green.

**Southwold
The Common 1896**

38629

These bonneted Victorian children seem to have been strategically placed on The Common by the photographer. The Common is another of Southwold's open spaces, which give the town a spacious air.

Southwold
The Beach 1919 69110
Nannies take their children for a stroll in their prams along the road overlooking Southwold's sandy beach.
The beach is still lined with wooden beach huts, as it was eighty years ago.

Southwold
From The Pier 1919 69119
This fine view of the front shows the Grand Hotel prominent on the right. Note the fishing boats hauled up on the beach, the wooden, wheeled bathing huts in the middle distance, and the lighthouse on North Green at the extreme left.

Suffolk Coast - Photographic Memories

Southwold ▶

Gun Hill 1919 69115
Gun Hill, a grassy eminence at the southern end of Southwold, takes its name from the six eighteen-pounder cannons which were presented to the town by the Duke of Cumberland in 1746 after the Battle of Culloden - the town had complained about its lack of defences. They can be seen behind the two women walking on the right.

◀ **Southwold
The Lighthouse 1919**
69120
The gleaming white lighthouse was erected in 1899 and stands amid some of the finest Georgian-style houses in the town at North Green. The building is Southwold's trademark, and is topped by a golden weather vane, making it a landmark for miles around.

◀ **Southwold
The Beach 1925**

77999

The fine array of spick and span, black and white, almost mock-Tudor, bathing huts on the beach await the first visitors of the season. Behind them on the clifftop are the hotels and guest houses where many of their occupants stayed.

Suffolk Coast - Photographic Memories

▼ **Southwold, East Green and the Lighthouse 1933** 85869
The public house just to the right of the lighthouse tower is the Sole Bay Inn, named after the bay to the north of the town where the sole was a common catch for Southwold's fishermen.

▼ **Southwold, The Coast Guard Station 1933** 85880
His Majesty's Coastguard stands proudly in his uniform at the entrance of the octagonal Coastguard Station. At this time he was kept busy because of Southwold's prime position as one of the major East Coast ports. Today, however, there is only an inshore rescue boat stationed on the Blyth estuary.

▲ **Thorpeness
The Beach 1922**
72586
Thorpeness, between Aldeburgh and Dunwich, was built around the old fishing hamlet of Thorpe, which takes it name from an old Danish word meaning a small settlement or hamlet. The 'ness' element, another old Scandinavian word, refers to the headland of Thorpe Ness, to the north of the village.

◄ **Thorpeness**
The Beach 1922 72588
The modern village of Thorpeness is largely the creation of Glencairn Stuart Ogilvie, the dramatist and author, who was a friend of Henry Irving. He built the model village in an eccentric mixture of styles, but mainly in a gloriously over-the-top mock-Tudor, as we can see here.

Suffolk Coast - Photographic Memories

▼ **Thorpeness, The Beach 1929** *82982*
This is a reminder of the village's maritime past, with fishing boats drawn up on the shingle. In the distance further down the beach, holidaymakers enjoy the sun and surf.

▼ **Thorpeness, The Sanctuary 1929** *82984*
The Sanctuary was one of Ogilvie's grandest creations, built in almost medieval style with a buttressed and half-timbered tower for a gateway. The building on the left, however, is pure Tudor in style, imitating neighbouring Aldeburgh's famous Moot Hall.

▲ **Thorpeness The Lake and Boats 1929** *82989*
The boathouse on the Meare at Thorpeness was a popular place of resort for holidaymakers in the late 1920s. The children in the boat in the centre anxiously wait for their parents to come, so they can set out on their trip.

◀ **Thorpeness**
The Lake 1929 *82987*
The lake at Thorpeness, known as the Meare, was also dug by Ogilvie as the centrepiece of his model village. It is only three feet deep, so the couple in the punt could cross it with ease.

◄ **Thorpeness**
The House in the Clouds
c1955 T38040
Thorpeness's most famous
building is undoubtedly
the House in the Clouds, on
the left of this photograph
taken from the track called
Uplands Road. Originally built
as a water tower, this 85ft tall
structure was later converted
to a most unusual house.
Opposite stands the white-
painted post mill, built in 1803
and moved to Thorpeness in
the 1920s, where it now serves
as an information centre.

◄ **Thorpeness**
The Estate Office
c1955 T38018
This was Ogilvie's Estate Office. Ogilvie's intention was to create a village 'for people who want to experience life as it was lived when England was Merrie England'. Note the horse and trap in the centre foreground, and the bicycle trailer on the extreme left.

▼ **Thorpeness**
From the Beach c1960
T38047
A regimented line of deserted black-painted beach huts dominates this view, probably taken in the winter. The white-painted villas and houses of the village fill the background.

◄ **Trimley**
The Village 1899 43249
As with many other Suffolk villages, there are two Trimleys. The twin villages on the main A45 Ipswich-Felixstowe road are named after the dedication of their respective parish churches, Trimley St Martin and Trimley St Mary. This photograph shows a still-unmetalled main road, with the Three Mariners Inn on the left.

◀ **Walberswick
The Church 1891**
28355
The ivy-covered ruins
of the grand 15th-
century parish church
of St Andrew started
its sad decline almost
immediately after its
completion in 1493.
But the magnificent
tower and chancel
survive, and are still
in use as the parish
church.

◀ **Trimley**
High Road c1950 T80001
This photograph shows the High Road through Trimley St Mary, with the Melton Rubber Works in the background, and the sign to Church Lane pointing to the right on the left of the photograph.

▼ **Walberswick**
The Footbridge 1892
29934
A footbridge leads across a creek to the quay. Moored up at the quay is a fishing boat, its LT designation showing that it was registered at nearby Lowestoft.

◀ **Walberswick**
From the River 1896
38635
Walberswick stands at the mouth of the River Blyth just across from the boatyards of Southwold, and was once, like so many of these quiet Suffolk coast villages, a thriving port. Note the flint-faced and pantiled barns or warehouses on the right and the village in the background.

Walberswick ▶
The Beach 1896
38636
The estuary of the River Blyth. Moored up in the centre of the picture is one of the famous red-sailed East Anglian or Thames sailing barges, which plied up and down this coast for centuries, carrying produce from the region to the capital.

◀ **Walberswick**
The Ferry 1900 45138
A stiff easterly wind straightens the flag flying alongside the terminus of Walberswick's ferry across the wide estuary of the River Blyth.

◄ **Walberswick
The Footbridge
1900** 45140
This is another
charming little
footbridge across
one of the many
small creeks which
drain into the River
Blyth from the
marshy ground to
the south of the
village. Note the
fine post mill above
the bridge on the
skyline at the left of
the photograph.

◀ **Walberswick The Green 1919** 69130 The wide village green at Walberswick is typical of many in this part of East Anglia. On the right, the village stores awaits its customers, while a couple on their bicycles enjoy a leisurely ride through the village and a little girl in the centre dismounts to gaze at the photographer.

◄ **Walberswick**
The Ferry 1919 69126
The steam-operated Blyth ferry in operation, with a horse and cart aboard. A mass of fishing nets and ropes are loaded onto a handcart in the foreground, and a Lowestoft-registered fishing boat - LT798 - is laid up on the riverbank.

▼ **Walberswick**
The River c1955 W7077
At the time when this photograph was taken, the leisure explosion had seen Walberswick and many other Suffolk coast villages experience a new lease of life as boating and yachting centres. These small boats are making good use of a brisk breeze as they head out to sea along the River Blyth.

◄ **Walberswick**
The Ferry c1960
W7021
A gaggle of handsome-looking white geese dabble among the shingle near the Walberswick ferry, on the left. By this time, Walberswick had become well established as a holiday and boating centre.

▼ **Walberswick, The Kissing Bridge c1960** W7022
A couple cross the romantically-named Kissing Bridge. It is one of
many of the village's footbridges, crossing the marshy creeks which
run into the River Blyth here.

▲ **Walton
The Village, 1899**
43244
The village of Walton
was merged into
Felixstowe Urban
District Council four
years before this
photograph was
taken; before this
it was a separate,
adjoining parish.
Walton is perhaps
best known for its
17th-century lock-up
beside the restored
village church.

◀ **Walton, The Village 1899** 43245
The only traffic is horses and carts, and on the left stand a row of pantile-roofed almshouses, typical of this part of East Anglia.

Walton, The Parish Church 1901 46694

The parish church, seen here from the south-west, had been largely rebuilt in the 1860s and 1890s, but it still contains an exceptional brass dating from 1459. The 17th-century village lock-up mentioned in picture No 43244 was retained as a bus shelter beside the churchyard.

Westleton, The Green c1950 W441002

A villager helps himself to a bucket of drinking water from one of no less than three village pumps on Westleton's spacious village green. In the background stands Westleton's fine old post mill, its sails still in situ.

Westleton, The Village c1950 W441008
Westleton is an archetypal English village, clustered around its green where medieval archers may once have practised. This view of the village, which lies about two miles inland from Dunwich, shows the cross-roads and the village war memorial enclosed by posts and chains in the background.

Westleton, The Green c1950 W441005
Another view of the Green, probably taken on the same day as picture No W441008 but in the opposite direction. Note the prominent advertising hoardings outside the village shop on the right, and the village's nonconformist chapel with the van parked outside in the centre.

Details from: Westleton, The Village c1950 W441008
and Westleton, The Green c1950 W441005

Westleton, The Mill c1950 W441006
Westleton had two windmills, the post mill seen on photograph No W441002, and this tower mill, minus its sail when this photograph was taken. Tower mills like this one were usually brick-built and stationary, the cap spinning round to catch the wind, while the whole of the post mill swung round on its central post.

Westleton, The White Horse c1950 W441003
The locally-brewed Adnams Ales from nearby Southwold were sold at the red-brick White Horse Inn at Westleton, just off the village green.

Suffolk Coast - Photographic Memories

▼ **Westleton, The Church c1950** W441007
One of Westleton's greatest glories is its beautiful but unpretentious 14th-century parish church of St Peter. It is doubly unusual, in a county of grand wool churches, in having no tower or spire and by having a thatched roof covering its nave and chancel.

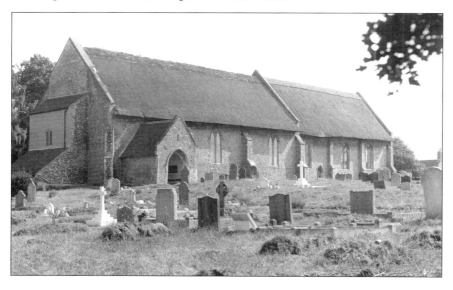

Woodbridge ▶
The Old Weighing
Station
New Street 1929
82959
New Street was new in the late Middle Ages, and its most unusual feature is this Old Weigh House. Probably built around the middle of the 17th century, it consists of a lever mechanism for weighing cartloads of produce drawn up in the street beneath. It was last commercially used in 1880.

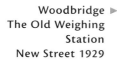

▲ **Woodbridge**
The Boat Station
1894 33372
A Thames sailing barge is moored up at the boat station, and others can be seen in the distance. These fine, flat-bottomed hulled vessels were then a common sight on the Suffolk and Essex coasts, taking goods to and from London and East Anglia.

◄ **Woodbridge
General View 1894** 33981
Woodbridge is undoubtedly one of the most attractive small towns in Suffolk, standing at the tidal limit of the River Deben, as this fine general view across the town shows. To the right can be seen one of Woodbridge's many famous old buildings, the Old Tide Mill. This photograph was taken near to the site of the great Saxon burial site of Sutton Hoo, across the river to the east of the town.

Woodbridge, The Thoroughfare 1906 53499
The influence of Dutch architecture so common on the East Coast can be seen in the fine, pinnacled façade of the bank building on the right; the Thoroughfare runs between New Street and Church Street. Note the horse and cart delivery van in the distance, and the gas street light on the extreme left.

▲ **Woodbridge**
Town Hall 1908 60685
Again the strong Dutch influence
can be seen in this photograph of
the magnificent Town or Shire Hall,
which was built around 1700, or
certainly early in the 18th century.
The tall hipped roof and curved
gables, stone quoins and elegant
double entrance staircases make
this one of Woodbridge's most
distinguished buildings.

◄ **Detail From:**
Woodbridge
Town Hall 1908 60685

Suffolk Coast - Photographic Memories

▼ **Woodbridge, The Old Tide Mill c1955** W128040

Woodbridge's most famous building is undoubtedly its Old Tide Mill, seen here from the banks of the Deben. The first mill was built on the site as early as 1170, but the one seen here (now restored into working condition, open to the public and painted a dazzling white) was constructed in the East Coast style of weatherboarding in the 1790s. It remained in operation, using the tidal flow of the Deben for its power, until 1957.

▼ **Wrentham, The Village c1955** W444010

Wrentham has always suffered from being on one of the major cross-roads of the county. It stands on the main A12 Ipswich-Lowestoft trunk road, and this photograph looks south at the roundabout where the B1127 Southwold-Beccles road crosses it.

▲ **Wrentham The Roundabout c1950** W444002
Another view of that busy roundabout, this time looking towards the centre of the village with the tall, red-brick spire of the Congregational Chapel, built in 1778, prominent in the centre of the photograph.

◀ **Wrentham**
A Thatched Cottage
c1955 W444023
Suffolk is a county of thatched cottages, and even thatched churches, as we saw at Westleton. This delightful cottage is a fine example of the thatcher's art, probably using the excellent Norfolk reeds which are generally accepted to be the best material for this task.

Wrentham, The Spread Eagle Hotel c1950 W444001
By the time this photograph was taken, the Spread Eagle Hotel had decided that the age of the motor car had truly arrived. It proudly advertised its car park by painting the words on its pantiled roof. Note the Dutch gable to the left.

Wrentham, The Horse and Groom c1950 W444004
The Horse and Groom was, on the other hand, still very much a country pub, overlooking the fields and depending on the locals and passing trade for its livelihood. Again, like so many buildings on the Suffolk coast, it had a pantiled roof.

Index

Southwold From the Air 1951 AF38320

The Francis Frith Collection publishes over 100 new titles each year. A selection of those currently available is listed below. For latest catalogue please contact The Francis Frith Collection.
Town Books 96 pages, approximately 75 photos. **County and Themed Books** 128 pages, approximately 135 photos (unless specified). Pocket Albums are miniature editions of Frith local history books 128 pages, approximately 95 photos.

Accrington Old and New
Alderley Edge and Wilmslow
Amersham, Chesham and Rickmansworth
Andover
Around Abergavenny
Around Alton
Aylesbury
Barnstaple
Bedford
Bedfordshire
Berkshire Living Memories
Berkshire Pocket Album
Blackpool Pocket Album
Bognor Regis
Bournemouth
Bradford
Bridgend
Bridport
Brighton and Hove
Bristol
Buckinghamshire
Calne Living Memories
Camberley Pocket Album
Canterbury Cathedral
Cardiff Old and New
Chatham and the Medway Towns
Chelmsford
Chepstow Then and Now
Cheshire
Cheshire Living Memories
Chester
Chesterfield
Chigwell
Christchurch
Churches of East Cornwall
Clevedon
Clitheroe
Corby Living Memories
Cornish Coast
Cornwall Living Memories
Cotswold Living Memories
Cotswold Pocket Album
Coulsdon, Chipstead and Woodmanstern
County Durham
Cromer, Sheringham and Holt
Dartmoor Pocket Album
Derby
Derbyshire
Derbyshire Living Memories
Devon
Devon Churches
Dorchester

Dorset Coast Pocket Album
Dorset Living Memories
Dorset Villages
Down the Dart
Down the Severn
Down the Thames
Dunmow, Thaxted and Finchingfield
Durham
East Anglia Pocket Album
East Devon
East Grinstead
Edinburgh
Ely and The Fens
Essex Pocket Album
Essex Second Selection
Essex: The London Boroughs
Exeter
Exmoor
Falmouth
Farnborough, Fleet and Aldershot
Folkestone
Frome
Furness and Cartmel Peninsulas
Glamorgan
Glasgow
Glastonbury
Gloucester
Gloucestershire
Greater Manchester
Guildford
Hailsham
Hampshire
Harrogate
Hastings and Bexhill
Haywards Heath Living Memories
Heads of the Valleys
Heart of Lancashire Pocket Album
Helston
Herefordshire
Horsham
Humberside Pocket Album
Huntingdon, St Neots and St Ives
Hythe, Romney Marsh and Ashford
Ilfracombe
Ipswich Pocket Album
Isle of Wight
Isle of Wight Living Memories
King's Lynn
Kingston upon Thames
Lake District Pocket Album
Lancashire Living Memories
Lancashire Villages

Available from your local bookshop or from the publisher

The Francis Frith Collection Titles (continued)

Lancaster, Morecambe and Heysham Pocket Album
Leeds Pocket Album
Leicester
Leicestershire
Lincolnshire Living Memoires
Lincolnshire Pocket Album
Liverpool and Merseyside
London Pocket Album
Ludlow
Maidenhead
Maidstone
Malmesbury
Manchester Pocket Album
Marlborough
Matlock
Merseyside Living Memories
Nantwich and Crewe
New Forest
Newbury Living Memories
Newquay to St Ives
North Devon Living Memories
North London
North Wales
North Yorkshire
Northamptonshire
Northumberland
Northwich
Nottingham
Nottinghamshire Pocket Album
Oakham
Odiham Then and Now
Oxford Pocket Album
Oxfordshire
Padstow
Pembrokeshire
Penzance
Petersfield Then and Now
Plymouth
Poole and Sandbanks
Preston Pocket Album
Ramsgate Old and New
Reading Pocket Album
Redditch Living Memories
Redhill to Reigate
Richmond
Ringwood
Rochdale
Romford Pocket Album
Salisbury Pocket Album
Scotland
Scottish Castles
Sevenoaks and Tonbridge
Sheffield and South Yorkshire Pocket Album
Shropshire
Somerset
South Devon Coast
South Devon Living Memories
South East London

Southampton Pocket Album
Southend Pocket Album
Southport
Southwold to Aldeburgh
Stourbridge Living Memories
Stratford upon Avon
Stroud
Suffolk
Suffolk Pocket Album
Surrey Living Memories
Sussex
Sutton
Swanage and Purbeck
Swansea Pocket Album
Swindon Living Memories
Taunton
Teignmouth
Tenby and Saundersfoot
Tiverton
Torbay
Truro
Uppingham
Villages of Kent
Villages of Surrey
Villages of Sussex Pocket Album
Wakefield and the Five Towns Living Memories
Warrington
Warwick
Warwickshire Pocket Album
Wellingborough Living Memories
Wells
Welsh Castles
West Midlands Pocket Album
West Wiltshire Towns
West Yorkshire
Weston-super-Mare
Weymouth
Widnes and Runcorn
Wiltshire Churches
Wiltshire Living Memories
Wiltshire Pocket Album
Wimborne
Winchester Pocket Album
Windermere
Windsor
Wirral
Wokingham and Bracknell
Woodbridge
Worcester
Worcestershire
Worcestershire Living Memories
Wyre Forest
York Pocket Album
Yorkshire
Yorkshire Coastal Memories
Yorkshire Dales
Yorkshire Revisited

See Frith books on the internet at www.francisfrith.com

FRITH PRODUCTS & SERVICES

Francis Frith would doubtless be pleased to know that the pioneering publishing venture he started in 1860 still continues today. Over a hundred and forty years later, The Francis Frith Collection continues in the same innovative tradition and is now one of the foremost publishers of vintage photographs in the world. Some of the current activities include:

INTERIOR DECORATION

Today Frith's photographs can be seen framed and as giant wall murals in thousands of pubs, restaurants, hotels, banks, retail stores and other public buildings throughout the country. In every case they enhance the unique local atmosphere of the places they depict and provide reminders of gentler days in an increasingly busy and frenetic world.

PRODUCT PROMOTIONS

Frith products are used by many major companies to promote the sales of their own products or to reinforce their own history and heritage. Frith promotions have been used by Hovis bread, Courage beers, Scots Porage Oats, Colman's mustard, Cadbury's foods, Mellow Birds coffee, Dunhill pipe tobacco, Guinness, and Bulmer's Cider.

GENEALOGY AND FAMILY HISTORY

As the interest in family history and roots grows world-wide, more and more people are turning to Frith's photographs of Great Britain for images of the towns, villages and streets where their ancestors lived; and, of course, photographs of the churches and chapels where their ancestors were christened, married and buried are an essential part of every genealogy tree and family album.

FRITH PRODUCTS

All Frith photographs are available Framed or just as Mounted Prints and Posters (size 23 x 16 inches). These may be ordered from the address below. Other products available are- Address Books, Calendars, Jigsaws, Canvas Prints, Coasters, Notelets and local and prestige books.

THE INTERNET

Already ninety thousand Frith photographs can be viewed and purchased on the internet through the Frith websites and a myriad of partner sites.

For more detailed information on Frith companies and products, look at this site:
www.francisfrith.com

See the complete list of Frith Books at: www.francisfrith.com

This web site is regularly updated with the latest list of publications from The Francis Frith Collection. If you wish to buy books relating to another part of the country that your local bookshop does not stock, you may purchase on-line.

For further information, trade, or author enquiries please contact us at the address below:
The Francis Frith Collection, Frith's Barn, Teffont, Salisbury, Wiltshire, England SP3 5QP.
Tel: +44 (0)1722 716 376 Fax: +44 (0)1722 716 881 Email: sales@francisfrith.co.uk

---

See Frith products on the internet at www.francisfrith.com

FREE PRINT OF YOUR CHOICE

Mounted Print
Overall size 14 x 11 inches (355 x 280mm)

Choose any Frith photograph in this book.
Simply complete the Voucher opposite and return it with your remittance for £3.50 (to cover postage and handling) and we will print the photograph of your choice in SEPIA (size 11 x 8 inches) and supply it in a cream mount with a burgundy rule line (overall size 14 x 11 inches).
Please note: aerial photographs and photographs with a reference number starting with a "Z" are not Frith photographs and cannot be supplied under this offer. Offer valid for delivery to one UK address only.

PLUS: Order additional Mounted Prints at HALF PRICE - £9.50 each (normally £19.00)
If you would like to order more Frith prints from this book, possibly as gifts for friends and family, you can buy them at half price (with no additional postage and handling costs).

PLUS: Have your Mounted Prints framed
For an extra £18.00 per print you can have your mounted print(s) framed in an elegant polished wood and gilt moulding, overall size 16 x 13 inches (no additional postage and handling required).

IMPORTANT!

These special prices are only available if you use this form to order. You must use the ORIGINAL VOUCHER on this page (no copies permitted). We can only despatch to one UK address. This offer cannot be combined with any other offer.

Send completed Voucher form to:
The Francis Frith Collection, Frith's Barn, Teffont, Salisbury, Wiltshire SP3 5QP

CHOOSE A PHOTOGRAPH FROM THIS BOOK

Voucher for **FREE** and Reduced Price Frith Prints

Please do not photocopy this voucher. Only the original is valid, so please fill it in, cut it out and return it to us with your order.

Picture ref no	Page no	Qty	Mounted @ £9.50	Framed + £18.00	Total Cost £
		1	Free of charge*	£	£
			£9.50	£	£
			£9.50	£	£
			£9.50	£	£
			£9.50	£	£
			£9.50	£	£

Please allow 28 days for delivery.
Offer available to one UK address only

* Post & handling	£3.50
Total Order Cost	£

Title of this book . . . .

I enclose a cheque/postal order for £ . . . . made payable to 'The Francis Frith Collection'

OR please debit my Mastercard / Visa / Maestro card, details below

Card Number

Issue No (Maestro only)   Valid from (Maestro)

Expires   Signature

Name Mr/Mrs/Ms . . . .

Address . . . .

. . . .

. . . .

. . . . Postcode . . . .

Daytime Tel No . . . .

Email . . . .

978-1-85937-610-2   Valid to 31/12/11

Free Print – see overleaf

Can you help us with information about any of the Frith photographs in this book?

We are gradually compiling an historical record for each of the photographs in the Frith archive. It is always fascinating to find out the names of the people shown in the pictures, as well as insights into the shops, buildings and other features depicted.

If you recognize anyone in the photographs in this book, or if you have information not already included in the author's caption, do let us know. We would love to hear from you, and will try to publish it in future books or articles.

An Invitation from The Francis Frith Collection to Share Your Memories

The 'Share Your Memories' feature of our website allows members of the public to add personal memories relating to the places featured in our photographs, or comment on others already added. Seeing a place from your past can rekindle forgotten or long held memories. Why not visit the website, find photographs of places you know well and add YOUR story for others to read and enjoy? We would love to hear from you!

www.francisfrith.com/memories

Our production team

Frith books are produced by a small dedicated team at offices in the converted Grade II listed 18th-century barn at Teffont near Salisbury, illustrated above. Most have worked with the Frith Collection for many years. All have in common one quality: they have a passion for the Frith Collection.

Frith Books and Gifts

We have a wide range of books and gifts available on our website utilising our photographic archive, many of which can be individually personalised.

www.francisfrith.com